SEARCH AND RESCUE TEAMS

ON THE SCENE

BY KARA L. LAUGHLIN

The Child's World®
childsworld.com

Published by The Child's World®
1980 Lookout Drive • Mankato, MN 56003-1705
800-599-READ • www.childsworld.com

Photographs: EB Adventure Photography/Shutterstock.com, cover, 1;
US Air National Guard/Major Geoff Legler, 5; US National Guard/Inyo County
Search and Rescue, 6; US National Park Service, 10, 15, 20; jasomtomo/
Shutterstock.com, 12; US National Guard/Major Kyle Key, 16; US National
Guard/Staff Sergeant Alex Baum, 18

ISBN 9781503855854 (Reinforced Library Binding)
ISBN 9781503856165 (Portable Document Format)
ISBN 9781503856400 (Online Multi-user eBook)
LCCN: 2021940171

Printed in the United States of America

TABLE OF
CONTENTS

FAST FACTS

What's the Job?

- Search and Rescue (SAR) teams drop everything at a moment's notice to find and save people who have been reported lost.

- SAR volunteers can get **certified** in many types of search and rescue operations. Some common types of SAR include **urban**, mountain, drone, wilderness, and SAR dog or horse teams.

- Some SAR teams work with US aid agencies. These teams get sent all over the world when disaster strikes.

- Many SAR teams also work in PSAR (Preventative Search and Rescue). They teach people how to be safe outdoors and avoid getting lost.

The Dangers

- Search and Rescue missions can be dangerous. SAR teams are often out in the wild and in bad weather. Team members search day and night in **remote** areas and places with dangerous animals.

- Urban SAR teams often work where buildings have collapsed. Some dangers they cope with are earthquake **aftershocks**, live electrical wires, and gas leaks.

Important Stats

- Most SAR team members are volunteers. They pay for their own training and equipment.

- The Armed Forces, Coast Guard, and many police and fire departments have SAR teams.

- Some SAR workers just do SAR. Many others do SAR as part of a bigger job.

- SAR teams spring into action! Coast Guard SAR teams must be ready within 30 minutes of being called, and on the scene within two hours.

- In general, 85 percent of all lost people are found within the first 12 hours. Ninety-seven percent are found within the first 24 hours.

Chapter 1

THE RIGHT PLACE AT THE RIGHT TIME

Lauren Knott shook her snowshoe and took another step. She was a youth member of the Marin Search and Rescue team. She was out training with her team. For Lauren, Search and Rescue was a way to give back to her community.

Her team held practices once a month to keep their skills sharp. They also met inside to learn new skills. Every rescue was different, and her SAR team needed to be prepared.

The snow on the mountain was melting in the early spring sun. Up ahead, the group had stopped. Lauren wondered why. Then she heard it. Crying. Screaming. The team followed the cries.

Soon they found where the cries were coming from. There in the snow of Tahoe National Forest stood a family: father, mother, brother. But someone else was there. The team heard her crying, but they could not see her.

◀ **Most SAR teams meet weekly and train in the field about once a month. Wilderness SAR team members have to carry all the tools and equipment they need in backpacks.**

The father told the team that his ten-year-old daughter, Samantha, had fallen 10 feet (3 meters) into an ice cave. She wasn't hurt, but she was cold and scared. Samantha was standing in an icy stream, and she couldn't get out.

The family had tried to pull her out with a hiking pole, but Samantha couldn't hold on. They stopped when they realized the cave might collapse and trap them all.

Samantha's dad, a firefighter, had called 911. But he knew it would take some time before that help arrived.

The SAR team got right to work. They worked carefully and quickly. They created a loop of rope and tossed it down to Samantha. Samantha slipped it under her arms. In 15 minutes, the team had hauled her out.

Samantha was cold and wet. She was out of the ice, but not out of danger. A team member checked her health. Samantha was not injured, but she had been standing in icy water for some time. She needed to warm up.

Lauren searched her SAR backpack. Every rescuer was required to carry a backpack with essentials. Lauren took out some warm clothes. Others helped Samantha out of her wet jacket and socks. Lauren put her knit hat on Samantha's head.

"That looks good on you," Lauren said.

The girl who had been scared and crying moments ago gave Lauren a smile.

The team got Samantha into dry socks and a warm, dry jacket. If the family had needed it, Lauren had food, water, blankets, and a flashlight, too.

Lauren looked around at her team. They had saved a life—on a training trip! The Marin SAR team had lived up to their motto: "Any time, anywhere, any weather."

WHAT'S IN THE PACK?

SAR team members must bring a backpack on their searches. Although the contents depend on the area, here is what's found in most packs:

- Blanket
- Compass
- Duct tape
- Extra clothes
- First aid kit
- Food
- Gloves
- Hat
- Headlamp (or flashlight)
- Heavy-duty trash bags
- Map
- Matches (or a lighter)
- Pocketknife
- Portable two-way radio
- Rain gear
- Water

Chapter 2

MOUNTAIN MIRACLE

Firefighter Mike Tussey was worried about Kenny Howard. Kenny was not quite two years old. He had gone missing from his backyard in Kentucky.

Soon after, a SAR team was on the job, starting a **grid search**. The **search coordinator** divided a map into squares. Every team searched a square. SAR teams from nearby towns came to help. As more people arrived, more squares were searched. The search continued. Teams from three states came to help. Still no Kenny.

Now the search was in its third day. Hundreds of people— professional and volunteer SAR teams—were searching for Kenny. Helicopters and drones searched from above. On the ground, horses carried searchers into rough **terrain**. Dogs tried to sniff him out.

◄ SAR teams often work in remote areas with steep terrain. It's important for crew members to keep their skills sharp and work well as a team.

▲ Search and rescue dogs can pick up the scent of people who are lost. SAR dogs can also help rescuers locate missing people after a natural disaster.

Mike hoped to find Kenny alive. But he knew after three days, there was not much hope. It had rained, which meant Kenny's clothes would be wet. At night, the weather was close to freezing. People died in conditions like that. For a toddler to survive would be a miracle.

Mike feared the rescue would become a **recovery mission**. Mike knew recovery missions were important. Finding a person's remains helped people to move on. Still, he hoped this case would have a happy ending.

That morning, SAR dog teams had followed a **scent trail** from Kenny's yard to a wild area nearby. Then they lost the scent. Mike was in that area now, working with a man named Clay, an expert in tracking and rough terrain SAR. If the little boy was in their area, they would find him.

The two men headed over a hill. Almost as soon as they did, they heard a cry. But the eight-person team was calling for Kenny and yelling updates to each other. Mike couldn't hear the cry.

"Hush up, everyone!" he called.

The SAR team got quiet. Mike listened. There it was again. A child's voice!

"I found him!" Mike cried. He took off running toward the voice. Clay was right behind him.

Mike and Clay pushed through thick grass and bushes. They came to a cliff face. There, about 50 feet (15 meters) above them, was a little blond face with blue eyes. Kenny! He was perched on a small flat area. Kenny was scratched, dirty, and barefoot—and alive!

The two men called in their location. Then they headed up to Kenny. Five minutes later, they were with him. Mike took a sport drink from his backpack. He gave it to Kenny, who drank and drank. When he finally had enough to drink, Kenny started asking for his mom and dad.

Mike was a brave hero. He was tough and strong. He was also a father who knew what it was like to be scared for his kids. Later that day, he would tell a reporter that at this moment, he was "bawling like a baby."

Soon the rest of the SAR team arrived. After a health check showed Kenny was OK, the team made a special carrier for him. They cut out holes in a backpack for his legs. The youngest member of their team got to carry Kenny out of the woods in the pack.

A helicopter arrived to take Kenny to a hospital. Mike Tussey watched the helicopter fly up in the air. Kenny would be in a warm bed soon. He would be with his mother and father again.

It felt like a miracle—a miracle the SAR teams made happen together.

A SAR worker signals a helicopter while ▶ talking to the flight crew on a radio.

Chapter 3

PLANE CRASH!

The April afternoon sun flashed on Mount Jupiter near Brinnon, Washington. In the bright snow below, a two-passenger plane balanced, half-buried, on the side of the icy mountain. Two men were inside. They were injured, cold, and afraid.

The plane's pilot had sent a distress call a little before 4 p.m. Several teams searched the area for two hours. At last, a SAR pilot spotted a flash of red. He went in closer. He could just make out a white shape against the snowy mountain. The SAR team had found the missing plane!

Forty minutes later, John Siedler was in a helicopter on the way to the crash site.

John was a chief flight **medic** for the US Navy's SAR team on Whidbey Island. John had been at the air station when the call for help came. The SAR team had a medic already, but since John was there when the call came in, he tagged along. It was a good thing he did.

◀ **A flight crew member from the US National Guard scans an area during a search and rescue mission in a remote location.**

▲ If a helicopter can't land during a rescue operation, SAR workers and the equipment they need must be lowered to the ground with ropes.

The helicopter pilots flew to the crash site. The plane was in the snow on the side of a steep mountain. There would be no way for the helicopter to land nearby. The medics would have to **rappel** down to the crash.

John dropped out of the helicopter with a **litter** dangling below him. It was now nearly 7 p.m. The sun would set in an hour. As he rappelled 75 feet (23 meters) down to the site of the crash, John tried to prepare himself for anything. Plane crash missions could be pretty grim.

John had seen plenty of crashes. John's team helped the US Navy with mountain rescues and medical evacuations. Search and Rescue was all they did. The unit had gone on almost 30 missions in the past year. The Navy kept them busy. Still, when non-Navy calls came in, the team helped when it could. Like with this plane crash.

John's spirits lifted when he saw the two survivors on the wing of the plane. They had gotten themselves out of the cockpit—a great sign.

The two medics moved toward the plane. They had to be careful. The mountain was covered in thick ice. Just walking was tricky. The plane's tail had snapped and was dangling in the air. The plane had a parachute, but it hadn't deployed. The men worried the swinging tail could set it off. That could cause an avalanche. If the parachute opened near the helicopter, it could get tangled in the rotors. They didn't want one crash to become two!

The medics got to work checking the survivors. One probably had a broken leg. The other had hurt his back. They both needed to warm up or they could die. The medics warmed them up. Then they strapped each man into a litter. A litter is like a long sled. It keeps people still when moving might harm them.

▲ A SAR team carries an injured person on a litter. Bringing missing people to safety is the goal of SAR missions.

The team carried each man to a spot below the helicopter. Down came the cable. One by one, they secured the litters to the cable. Each man was hoisted into the air and pulled into the helicopter. Lastly, the medics went up. The pilot flew the men to safety.

These were the days that reminded John why he did the work. He'd put in 1,000 hours just to work for the Whidbey Island SAR team. He was on call 24/7.

People in SAR teams might leave a birthday party or barbecue to look for a missing child. They spend entire days and nights cold and wet—or sweating and thirsty. They sometimes go days without sleeping. Sometimes they never find the people they are looking for.

And then there are days like this one. Days when all the training and all they gave up are worth it. Days when they save lives.

THINK ABOUT IT

- If you were on a SAR team, what would be the hardest part for you? What part do you think you would like best?

- Searches change based on the people SAR teams are trying to find. The team knew a toddler like Kenny might move around a lot, so they kept searching the same areas. What changes should a team make if they are searching for a deaf person? What about someone in a wheelchair? Can you think of other people who might need to be looked for in a special way?

- SAR volunteers bring many skills to a search. Some speak different languages. Some know a lot about animals in the area. Do you know someone with a special skill that might help a SAR team? In what kind of search might they be especially helpful?

GLOSSARY

aftershocks (AFF-tur-shoks): An aftershock is a smaller earthquake that follows the main earthquake.

certified (SUR-tih-fide): Certified means being officially approved and qualified to perform a certain skill or job.

grid search (GRID SURCH): A grid search is a type of search where each team is given a precise area on a map.

litter (LIT-tur): A litter is lightweight sled made of metal and plastic. It is used to carry people to safety.

medic (MED-ik): A medic refers to someone who is trained to give first aid and minor medical care.

rappel (ruh-PELL): To rappel is to use a rope or cable and a harness to move from a high place to the ground.

recovery mission (ree-KUH-vuh-ree MISH-un): A recovery mission is when the SAR team's task is to find a body.

remote (rih-MOHT): A place that is far from people is remote.

scent trail (SENT TRAYL): A scent trail is the scent a person leaves. Dogs can sniff out and follow scent trails.

search coordinator (SURCH koh-OR-dih-nay-tur): A search coordinator is the person who runs a SAR operation.

terrain (tuh-RAYN): Terrain is a stretch of land. SAR teams are prepared to work in different types of terrain.

urban (UR-bun): Urban refers to a city location. Urban SAR teams often work in areas where a building has collapsed.

TO LEARN MORE

Books

Decker, William. *Getting Rescued in the Wild*. New York, NY: PowerKids, 2016.

Miller, Mirella S. *Search and Rescue Dogs on the Job*. Mankato, MN: The Child's World, 2017.

Spilsbury, Louise. *Search and Rescue Pilot*. New York, NY: Rosen, 2016.

Websites

Visit our website for links about Search and Rescue teams: childsworld.com/links

Note to Parents, Teachers, and Librarians: We routinely verify our Web links to make sure they are safe and active sites. So encourage your readers to check them out!

SELECTED BIBLIOGRAPHY

Esteban, Michelle. "NAS Whidbey Island Search & Rescue Crew Shares How They Found Plane Crash Survivors." *KOMO News*. April 3, 2017. https://komonews.com.

Jacobo, Julia. "'I Was Bawling like a Baby,' Says Firefighter Who Heard Cries of Kentucky Toddler Missing for 3 Days in the Woods." *ABC News*. May 16, 2019. https://abcnews.go.com.

Silverstein, Nikki. "Hero & Zero: Search and Rescue Heroes." *Pacific Sun*. March 2, 2016. https://pacificsun.com.

WKYT News Staff. "Magoffin County Toddler in 'Exceptionally Good' Condition after Being Found." WKYT Stands for Kentucky. May 16, 2019. https://www.wkyt.com.

INDEX

ABOUT THE AUTHOR

Kara L. Laughlin is the author of more than 60 nonfiction books for kids. She lives in Northern Virginia with her husband, three teenagers, and a dog named Vinny.